SCHOLASTIC

Adorable Wearables

That Teach About the Human Body

by Donald M. Silver and Patricia J. Wynne

NEW YORK • TORONTO • LONDON • AUCKLAND • SYDNEY
MEXICO CITY • NEW DELHI • HONG KONG • BUENOS AIRES

Teaching *Resources*

With this book, we honor Ruby Gandy Mitchell
PJW and DMS

"Eyes to See" and "Finger Wise" copyright © 1999 by Mary Sullivan. Reprinted by permission of the author.

Cover design by Maria Lilja
Cover photo by James Levin/Studio Ten
Cover and interior artwork by Patricia J. Wynne
Interior design by Holly Grundon

ISBN: 0-439-22269-9
Copyright © 2005 by Donald M. Silver and Patricia J. Wynne

Contents

Introduction

elcome to *Adorable Wearables That Teach About the Human Body*. The wearable models, background information, and lessons in this book have been designed to help motivate and guide young children toward understanding key concepts about the human body.

Tapping students' natural curiosity, the 12 wearables and the learning activities that complement them will let children learn first-hand what different parts of the body look like, what they're named, where exactly they're located, and what they do in the simplest terms. This will lay the foundation for a deeper understanding about the human body later on in school.

As they make, wear, and manipulate the wearables, children will be sharpening their skills in predicting, observing, comparing, and reasoning. What's more, they will be building essential vocabulary and practicing key language skills.

The concepts presented meet a number of the National Science Education Content Standards, the criteria that guide the content of science teaching and learning in this country. The chart on page 5 shows how the topics in this book correlate with several Content Standards for young children.

What's Inside

The wearable in each lesson focuses on a particular body part or system. Featured within each lesson are the following features:

Wearable Illustration

This picture shows how the finished wearable looks. It can be helpful to use as a reference when making the wearable.

Body Basics for the Teacher

This simple, easy-to-follow information provides background on the topic, for you, the teacher. Refer to some or all of this information when teaching the model, depending on the learning level of students and the kinds of questions they ask.

Materials

A complete list of everything you'll need for making the wearable and teaching the lesson.

Making the Wearable

These are easy-to-follow instructions with diagrams for assembling the wearables. (See Helpful Hints for Making the Wearables, page 6, for an overview.)

Sensitivity to Differences

When learning about the human body, children are bound to compare their physical similarities and differences. As you teach the lessons in this book, stress to children that while these differences are normal and help make each of us unique, people are more like one another than different from one another.

Words to Use

Here you'll find key vocabulary related to the lesson's topic and concepts. Use some or all of these words with the Teaching With the Wearable section, depending on the level of your students.

Teaching With the Wearable

This section provides a step-by-step lesson map for using the wearable to teach the lesson's main concepts.

Building Vocabulary

For children who are ready for a greater challenge, this section includes additional terms to introduce, plus ideas for boosting children's oral language.

Naïve Conceptions

This feature highlights ways in which young children might interpret or understand how different parts of their bodies work. It is important to note that even when presented with counter evidence, young children tend to hang on to these "naïve conceptions." The lessons and activities in this book provide the basis for a more in-depth understanding of the human body later on in school.

Body Bits

These bits of information offer unusual facts about the human body that will fascinate children.

Book Break

Use the books suggested here to complement and build on the lesson's concepts.

Explore More!

Extend learning with related activities that include short, simple science or math explorations, poems, games, songs, and more.

National Science Education
Content Standards
(Grades K-4)

Life Science

The Characteristics of Organisms:

❂ Organisms, including humans, have basic needs, such as air, water, and food.

❂ All organisms have specific structures that serve different functions in growth and survival. Humans have specialized body structures for walking, thinking, seeing, and talking, for example.

❂ The behavior of individual organisms is influenced by internal cues, such as hunger or pain, and by external cues, such as sounds, smells, or changes in temperature. Humans, as well as other organisms, have senses that help them detect these cues.

Science in Personal and Social Perspectives

Personal Health:

❂ Regular exercise is important to maintain and improve health. The benefits of physical fitness include having energy and strength for everyday activities, healthy muscle tone, and a strong heart, lungs, and bones.

❂ Personal care, such as dental hygiene, is important to maintain and improve health.

❂ For safe living, certain safety precautions must be taken.

❂ Food provides the energy and nutrients needed for growth and development.

From the *National Science Education Standards* published by the National Research Council (National Academy Press, 1996).

5

Getting Started . . . and Wrapping Up

Before making the first wearable with children, find out what they already know and what they would like to know about how their bodies work. After teaching with the wearables, invite children to share what they have learned. On chart paper, write some of the following prompts and encourage children to complete them.

Something inside me I learned about is _____.

Something on my outside that I learned about is _____.

I learned that my body can _____.

To take care of myself I learned to _____.

Something else I would like to learn about the human body is _____.

Helpful Hints for Making The Wearables

☀ The thickest black lines on the reproducible pages are CUT lines.

☀ Dotted lines on the reproducible pages are FOLD lines.

☀ Some wearables have slits or small windows to cut out. An easy way to make them is to fold the paper at a right angle to the solid cut lines. Then snip along the lines from the crease of the fold.

☀ Glue sticks can often be substituted for tape. However, some situations involving flaps require tape.

☀ Some wearables are more challenging to assemble than others. Read the Making the Wearable section beforehand and make the wearable yourself to determine if it's appropriate for children to do on their own. You can opt instead to make the wearable yourself and use it as a classroom demonstration tool.

☀ If a single wearable will be handled a great deal, consider creating it from heavier paper. Simply paste the reproducible page onto construction paper before beginning assembly.

Brain Hat

Children make hats
that show what the brain
looks like and what it does.

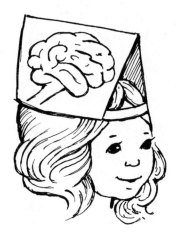

Body Basics for the Teacher

❋ The *brain* is located inside the skull. It is the control center for the entire body.

❋ The brain has three main parts: the *cerebrum*, the *cerebellum*, and the *brain stem*. Each part controls different aspects of the body.

❋ The cerebrum is the largest brain part. Thinking, dreaming, and remembering are organized here. The cerebrum also contains control centers for seeing, hearing, smelling, tasting, feeling/touch, and movement.

❋ The cerebellum helps make sure muscles work together smoothly. It also controls balance.

❋ The brain stem connects the brain to the *spinal cord*. The brain stem monitors breathing, blood pressure, and other basic body functions.

Materials

❋ Brain Hat pattern, page 10
❋ scissors
❋ tape
❋ paper strips, 2 by 6 inches
❋ crayons, colored pencils, or markers (optional)

Words to Use

hearing
moving
seeing
smelling
tasting
touching
think
dream
learn
remember

Making the Wearable

1. Photocopy page 10. Fold the page in half along the dotted line.

2. Cut out the Brain Hat along the outer solid line.

3. Tape the Brain Hat together at the back.

4. Fit the hat to each child's head by taping the paper strip between the open edges at the front of the hat.

Teaching With the Wearable

1. Before children put on their Brain Hats, find out what they know about the brain. Ask questions such as, "Where is your brain?" and "What does your brain do?" Explain that just like a computer, the brain receives and stores information through the eyes, ears, mouth, skin, and other parts of the body. It receives information about what goes on inside and outside the body. Then it sends messages to parts of the body and tells them what to do. The brain helps us walk and talk, eat and breathe, think, dream, have feelings, and remember.

2. Help children find the word *sight* which is printed on one side of the Brain Hat. Ask them to name the part of the body the brain works with to help us see. (*eyes*) Record this information on a sheet of chart paper.

3. Repeat this procedure with the other labels. (*touch, skin; hearing, ears; smell and taste, nose and tongue*) Children can color each part of the brain a different color, if desired.

4. Invite students to don their Brain Hats. Then, starting with the first words on the chart (*touch, skin*, for example), ask children to name things that we can do thanks to that part of our brain. (*feel a soft kitten, warmth of a hot day, a scratchy sweater, a rough rock*, and so on)

Building Vocabulary

For children who are ready to learn more, explain that tiny *nerves* that are as thin as hairs carry messages from the brain to the rest of the body. Reinforce the idea that the brain is our body's control center by playing a variation of Simon Says. The game will also help build directionality and give children practice using vocabulary for different body parts. Let children take turns being the caller. Have them replace the familiar words, "Simon Says to . . ." with "Your brain says to wiggle your left foot," for example.

Body Bits

It takes less than a split second for your brain to send a message to your big toe!

Naïve Conceptions

Children may have difficulty understanding the connection between the brain and the senses, or how the brain helps our bodies to perform various activities such as walking and breathing. This lesson lays the foundation for a more complex understanding later on in school.

Explore More!

Our Five Senses Collaborative Book

Reinforce the connection between the brain and the senses by having children make a class collaborative book. At the top of large sheets of construction paper, write the following sentence frame, with the appropriate variation for each sense. *The brain helps the eyes to see. We see _____.* Then divide the class into five groups, one for each sense. Invite each group to cut out pictures from old magazines or catalogs, or draw pictures that depict things related to its designated sense. Then help children complete the sentence frame with words that describe the pictures. Add extra pages as needed. Add a cover (invite each group to contribute to the cover by adding design elements related to its sense) and bind the book with O-rings or brass fasteners. Share the book as a class and then place it in your classroom library for children to read on their own.

Hard Heads

Help children understand the important role our skulls play in protecting our brains. First ask children to press their hands on their heads and then lightly tap them. How does the head feel? (*hard*) Ask children if they know what this part of the body is called. (*the skull*) Then divide the class into small groups.

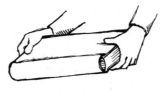

Give each group two balls of soft clay. Tell them to pretend that these are brains. Direct them to put one "brain" ball in a small plastic bag and the other under the plastic bowl.

Have them drop a book on each ball. What happens to each brain? (*The brain in the bag gets squashed; the brain under the bowl stays safe.*) Remind children that this is a science investigation and that they should never really drop heavy things on anyone's head. Ask children to feel their skulls again. How are the bowls like their skulls? What conclusions can they draw about what their skulls do?

As a followup, discuss the importance of wearing bike helmets. Explain that although our skulls offer protection, we can still hurt our heads if we fall off a bike. A bike helmet offers extra protection for both the skull and the brain.

Teaching Tip

For more about the sensory organs, see Vision Goggles, page 11; "Hear" Muffs, page 16; Skin and Hair Headband, page 22; and Teeth-and-Tongue Puppet, page 54.

Book Break

Share books about the brain and the five senses to help children explore these topics. Engaging titles, just right for young readers follow:

How Does Your Brain Work? by Don L. Curry (Children's Press, 2004)

Brain by Ann Sandeman (Copper Beech Books, 1996)

Me and My Senses by Joan Sweeney (Random House, 2003)

My Five Senses by Aliki (HarperCollins, 1962; revised 1989)

You Can't Taste a Pickle With Your Ear by Harriet Ziefert (Handprint Books, 2002).

Brain Hat Pattern

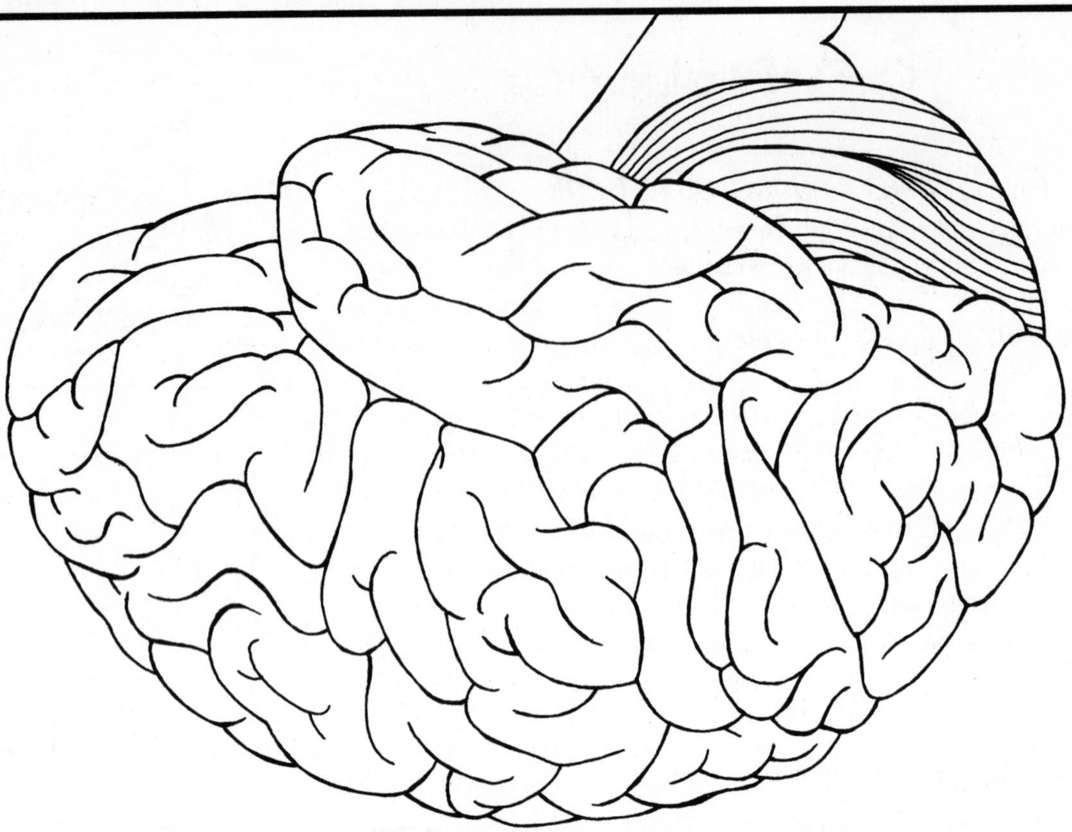

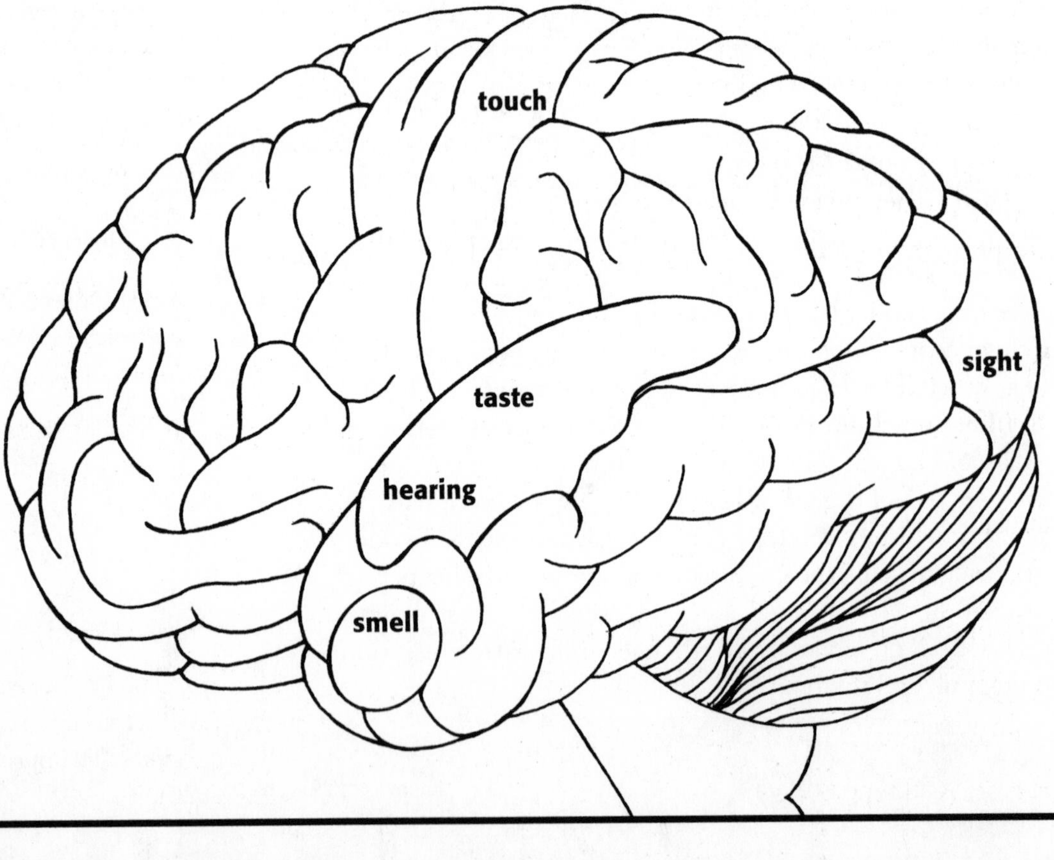

touch

taste

hearing

smell

sight

Adorable Wearables That Teach About the Human Body   Scholastic Teaching Resources

Vision Goggles

Children make goggles to learn about the parts of their eyes.

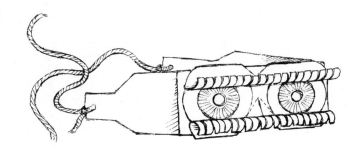

Body Basics for the Teacher

☀ *Eyelids* and *eyelashes* help keep dust and dirt out of the eyes.

☀ Every time we blink, the eyelids spread tears over each eye. Tears wash away dirt and help kill germs. They also help keep eyes moist.

☀ Tears are produced in *tear glands* above the eyes. Tears, made of water, flow across the eye and drain through *tear ducts* into the nose. The openings to the ducts are the small holes that are visible on the inner corners of the eyelids.

☀ We see when light enters our eyes. Light first passes through the clear layer in front of the eye which is called the *cornea* and then it passes through the *lens.* (For simplicity, neither is shown on the wearable.)

☀ Light then travels through the *pupil,* an opening in the colored part of the eye which is called the *iris.* The iris is made up of a ring of muscles that can relax or tighten to change the size of the pupil depending on the amount of light present. In dim light, the pupil expands to let in more light. In bright light, the iris tightens to make the pupil smaller.

☀ The light then reaches the *retina*—a light-sensitive layer at the back of the eye. The retina changes the light messages into electrical signals, which travel along the *optic nerve* to the *brain.* The brain then interprets the signals as an image that we see and understand.

Words to Use

eyelid
eyelashes
tear ducts
iris
pupil

Materials

☀ Vision Goggles patterns, page 15

☀ scissors

☀ hole punch

☀ tape

☀ two pieces of yarn or ribbon, each about 14 inches long

☀ hand mirrors

☀ crayons, colored pencils, or markers (optional)

☀ Brain Hat, page 10 (optional)

Making the Wearable

1. Photocopy page 15. Cut out the three patterns along the outer solid lines. Also cut along the solid lines on the eyelid pattern to create fringe-like eyelashes, and between the two eyeballs.

2. Roll the eyelashes around a pencil to curl them.

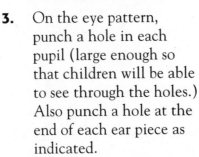

3. On the eye pattern, punch a hole in each pupil (large enough so that children will be able to see through the holes.) Also punch a hole at the end of each ear piece as indicated.

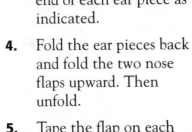

4. Fold the ear pieces back and fold the two nose flaps upward. Then unfold.

5. Tape the flap on each upper eyelid to the back of the eye pattern, as shown. Do the same with the lower eyelids.

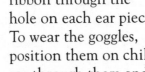

6. Fold down the upper eyelids and fold up the lower lids.

7. Tie a piece of yarn or ribbon through the hole on each ear piece. To wear the goggles, position them on children's faces so they can see through them and then tie the strings together in the back of the head.

Teaching With the Wearable

1. Discuss how different parts of our bodies help us make observations about our environment—to see, hear, feel, taste, and smell. Then ask children to point to the parts of their bodies that help them see. Ask: "How have you used your eyes today?"

2. Have children examine their goggles before putting them on. First point out the eyelids and let children open and close them. Then ask children to turn to each other and examine each other's eyelids and the area around them. What do they notice? (*they're made of soft skin; they open and close over the eyes; eyelashes grow out of them*) Ask, "What do you think your eyelids do?" Guide children to understand that our eyelids and lashes help keep dust and dirt out of our eyes and that we can close our eyelids to keep out light when we sleep.

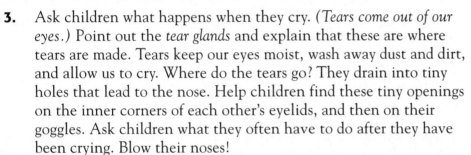

Tear glands

Tear ducts

3. Ask children what happens when they cry. (*Tears come out of our eyes.*) Point out the *tear glands* and explain that these are where tears are made. Tears keep our eyes moist, wash away dust and dirt, and allow us to cry. Where do the tears go? They drain into tiny holes that lead to the nose. Help children find these tiny openings on the inner corners of each other's eyelids, and then on their goggles. Ask children what they often have to do after they have been crying. Blow their noses!

4. Have children open the eyelids on their goggles. Point out the white part, the pupil, and the iris on each eye. Give each child (or pair of children) a hand mirror. What colors are the eyes of children in the class? Tell children to look in the mirror to see the color of their irises and then color the irises on their goggles the same color.

5. Invite children to wear their goggles. (Optional: Have children put on their Brain Hats, too.) Explain that the black circle, called the *pupil*, is actually an opening where light enters the eye so we can see things. The *iris*, the colored circle, opens and closes to change the size of the pupil. This allows the right amount of light to enter the eye. The light then passes to the back of the eye which in turn sends these light messages to the brain. If children have put on their Brain Hats, ask them why they think they are wearing them. (*The brain figures out what we are seeing.*)

Body Bits

We blink automatically—about 20 times in a minute. (Invite children to count their blinking rate while you time them for 60 seconds!)

Naïve Conceptions

Children may think that the pupil is a solid black circle, rather than an opening in the eye through which light can enter.

Book Break

Arthur's Eyes by Marc Brown (Little, Brown, 1979) Arthur's friends make fun of him when he gets glasses. So Arthur tries to lose his new specs. But when he discovers that his teacher wears the same kind, and that he can now read the board and score baskets in gym class—he feels much better!

Seeing by Sharon Gordon (Children's Press, 2002) Part of the Rookie Read-About Health series, this book describes, in simple terms, the features of the eyes and how they work. Includes colorful photos and clear diagrams.

••●● **Explore** More! ●●••

Close-up on Pupils

Invite children to see for themselves how their pupils change when light changes. Pair up children and give each pair a hand mirror. First ask children to take turns looking closely at their eyes. What details do they notice? (*red lines—blood vessels—on the white part of the eyes, different colors in the iris, iris may have a darker outer ring around it, black pupil*) Ask them to notice the size of the pupil. Then have one partner in each pair shut both eyes tightly and cover them with his or her hands while the other partner slowly counts to 20. Tell the first partners to open both eyes and look into the mirror to observe their pupils. Children should see that their pupil has grown larger and then gets smaller when exposed to the light. Have partners switch roles.

Eyes to See

On chart paper, copy the poem below. Read the poem together and then ask children to name things that they were lucky to see today. Write a class poem that begins with the first line of the poem and list children's responses.

Eyes to See

What luck that we have eyes to see:
The morning light,
The stars at night,
The blueness of the sea.

What luck that we have eyes to see:
The gentle deer,
Her fawn so near,
All creatures wild and free.

What luck that we have eyes to see:
The sun above,
The ones we love,
How lucky can we be!

—Mary Sullivan

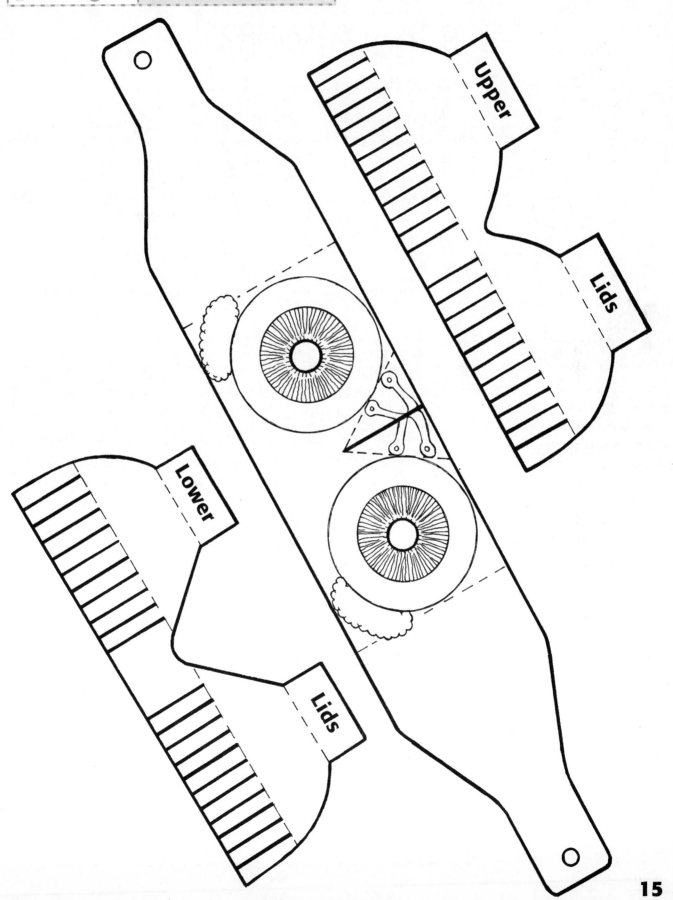

"Hear" Muffs

Children wear earmuffs with flaps
to learn about the outsides
and insides of the ears.

Body Basics for the Teacher

☀ All sounds start as *vibrations* (rapid back-and-forth movements) in the air.

☀ The outer, visible part of the ear collects and directs sound vibrations through the *ear canal*.

☀ The vibrations cause the *eardrum*, a small membrane that looks like the top of a drum, to vibrate.

☀ The vibrations pass from the eardrum through the three tiny bones in the middle ear. As these bones vibrate, they cause a liquid in the spiral-shaped *cochlea* (KOH-clee-uh) to move.

☀ *Nerves* in the cochlea pick up on this movement and send hearing messages to the *brain*. The brain figures out what we hear.

Materials

☀ "Hear" Muff patterns, pages 20–21

☀ scissors

☀ hole punch

☀ tape

☀ two pieces of yarn or ribbon, each about 14 inches long

☀ crayons, colored pencils, or markers (optional)

☀ Brain Hat, page 10 (optional)

Words to Use

sounds
ear
eardrum
ear bones
cochlea

Making the Wearable

1. Photocopy pages 20–21. Cut out the four patterns, and color the parts, if desired.

2. Fold each ear piece accordion-style along the dotted lines so that the outer ear flap is on top.

3. Punch a hole in the center of each outer ear flap.

4. Tape the tab on the left ear to its corresponding band piece. Do the same with the left ear.

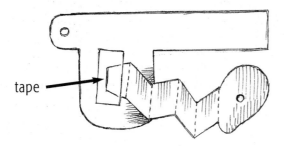

tape

5. Tape the edges of the two band patterns together as shown.

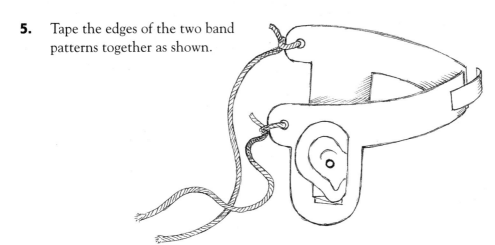

6. Punch a hole at the end of each band as indicated. Tie a piece of yarn or ribbon through each hole.

7. To wear the "Hear" Muffs, position the band across children's heads and tie in the back of the head with the yarn or ribbon.

17

Book Break

Help children explore the different sounds in their world with these books:

Listen to the City by Rachel Isadora (Putnam 2002).

Mara in the Morning by C.B. Christiansen (Simon & Schuster, 1991)

The Sound of Day, The Sound of Night by Mary O'Neill (Farrar, Straus & Giroux, 2003)

Teaching With the Wearable

1. Ask children to describe some of the sounds they heard on the way to school this morning. (*for instance, cars honking, people talking, radio playing*) Then discuss how hearing affects children's lives. For example, you might ask, "Can you tell about a time when you were glad you could hear?" or "Why is hearing important?" (*a car honking may alert us to get out of the way, talking lets us communicate with each other, hearing music is enjoyable, and so on*)

2. "What part of your body helps you hear?" (*ears*) Tell children that they are going to learn about how their ears help them hear sounds. Let children feel their own outer ears, and then observe a classmate's ears. Ask them what they notice about the outer ear. (*it sticks out; it's curved; there is an opening in it*) Ask: "How might the shape of your ears help you hear?" (*the shape of the outer ear helps catch sounds; the opening allows sounds to enter our body*)

3. Invite children to try on their "Hear" Muffs. Have them pair up and look at each other's models. Point out the outer part of the ear on the model and then have children lift the flaps to see the *eardrum*, the three tiny *ear bones*, and the spiral-shaped *cochlea*. Explain that the insides of the ear shown on the model have been enlarged so that children can see them easily. In reality, this part of the ear is only about one inch long.

4. Help children track the path of sound through the "Hear" Muff model. Explain that when something makes a sound (*for example, a person speaks or a dog barks*), the sound messages travel through the parts of the ear to our brain, which figures out what we are hearing. Optional: Have children put on their Brain Hats to emphasize this point.

Body Bits

Special structures in the inner ear help us to maintain our balance.

Naïve Conceptions

Children may believe that the outer part of the ear is what allows them to hear. Exploring the model will help them begin to build an understanding of the workings of the inner ear.

···●● **Explore** More! ●●···

Sound Collection Walk

Take your class on a "sound collection" walk. On notepads, encourage children to record the sounds they hear. Back in the classroom, start a word wall of descriptive words for the different sounds they collected (for example, *bang, clank, honk, crunch, buzz, boom*) You might invite children to group words into different categories such as quiet/noisy sounds, pleasant/unpleasant sounds, sounds made by living/nonliving things, and so on. Children may also enjoy using the word lists to write "sound" poems individually or in groups.

Rabbit Ears

Rabbits and other animals with excellent hearing have larger ears to better capture sounds. They can also point their ears in different directions to zero in on important sounds. Show children a picture of a rabbit. Ask them to describe its ears. How are its ears different from theirs? Ask children if they think a rabbit's ears might work differently than human ears. Then let them investigate to find out: For each child, cut a large paper cup in half . Have children hold the cup halves up to their ears. How do the cups change how they hear? (*sounds seem louder*). Ask children how they think this happens. (*The cups collect and direct sounds into the ears.*) How might big ears help a rabbit? (*They give a rabbit excellent hearing and help keep it safe from enemies.*)

Safety Note
Remind children never to shout into someone's ear and never to put anything directly in the ear.

One Ear or Two?

Why do we have two ears instead of just one? Let children discover this for themselves. Have a child sit in a chair with eyes closed. Another child stands and claps his or her hands in different locations (above, below, to the side, and so on) around the listener's head, as the listener keeps his or her head still. The listener tries to identify where the sound is coming from. Repeat the activity, but this time have the listener cover one ear. How well can the listener tell where the sounds are coming from now? (*It will be more difficult.*) How does having two ears help us figure out where sounds are coming from?

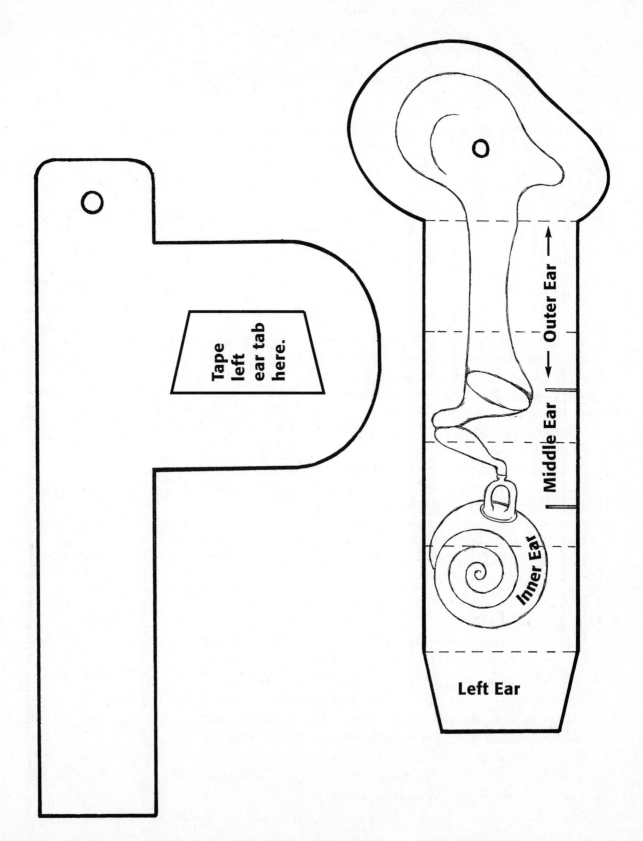

Tape
left
ear tab
here.

Outer Ear

Middle Ear

Inner Ear

Left Ear

Adorable Wearables That Teach About the Human Body   Scholastic Teaching Resources

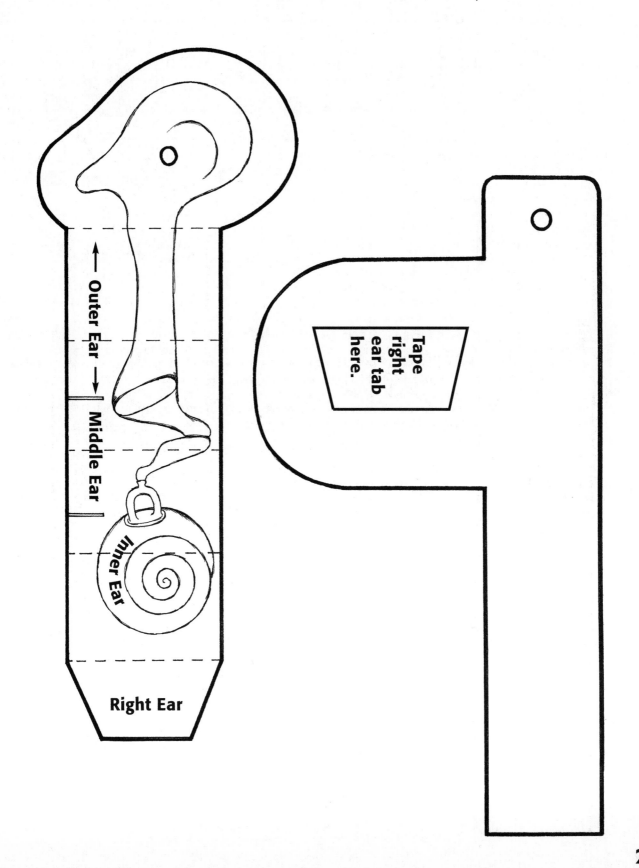

Outer Ear

Middle Ear

Inner Ear

Right Ear

Tape
right
ear tab
here.

Skin & Hair Headband

Children make headbands to learn about their skin and the hair that grows out of it.

Body Basics for the Teacher

❋ The skin covers and protects the skeleton, muscles, and organs in the body. It also helps keep out harmful germs.

❋ We use our skin to sense the world around us through touch. *Nerves* in skin (not shown on the model) send touch messages to the brain allowing us to feel warmth, cold, pressure, and pain.

❋ Skin has two main layers. The top layer, the *epidermis*, is as thin as a sheet of paper.

❋ The lower layer, the *dermis*, is thicker and filled with nerves that feel pressure and temperature.

❋ The dermis also contains glands that produce oil and sweat. Oil moisturizes the skin and hair; sweat helps cool our bodies as it evaporates through *pores* in the skin's surface.

❋ Hair starts growing out of *follicles* in the dermis. By the time it grows long enough to come out of the epidermis, the hair cells are dead. This is why it does not hurt when hair is cut.

❋ Fingernails and toenails are also part of our skin. Like hair, when nails grow out of the skin, the cells are dead and we have no feeling in them.

❋ The colors of skin and hair are determined by the amount of pigment, or *melanin*, they contain. Melanin helps to protect the skin from the sun. People with darker complexions have more melanin in their skin. Strong sunlight can cause the skin of people with lighter complexions to redden, tan, or freckle.

Words to Use

skin
protect
color
hair
eyebrows
eyelashes
oil
waterproof
sweat

Materials

- ☼ Skin and Hair Headband pattern, page 26
- ☼ scissors
- ☼ tape
- ☼ crayons, colored pencils, or markers (optional)
- ☼ hand lenses
- ☼ eyedropper and water
- ☼ assorted objects with different textures and shapes (sandpaper, rocks, stuffed animal, cotton ball, block, buttons)
- ☼ Brain Hat, page 10 (optional)

Making the Wearable

1. Make two copies of page 26 for each child and cut out the patterns.

2. Invite children to color the hair and skin, as desired.

3. Have children tape the edges of the patterns together. Then fit them to children's heads and tape closed.

Teaching With the Wearable

1. Ask children to share what they notice about their skin. (*different colors, some skin has freckles, wrinkles on fingers and knees, lines on fingers and palms, thicker on feet, and so on*) Pass out hand lenses so they can get a close-up look. Then invite children to wear their headbands. Have them look at each other's headbands and ask them to describe what they see. (Explain that the skin and hair under the hand lenses, and illustrated on the headbands, look bigger than they really are.)

2. Point out the two skin layers. In which layer does hair start growing? (*the lower layer*) Then ask children to name places where hair grows on their bodies and what it is like. (*head, eyebrows, eyelashes, arms*) Discuss ways hair helps the body. (*head hair keeps us warm; eyebrows and eyelashes keep dust and dirt out of our eyes*)

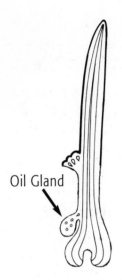

Oil Gland

Body Bits

How long does it take a hair to grow one inch? About two months!

Sensitivity to Differences

As you teach this lesson, stress to children that while differences in hair and skin color are normal and help make each of us unique, people are more like one another than different from one another.

3. Ask children to look around and then describe what the hair of children in the class is like. Discuss similarities and differences in length, color, and texture.

4. On the wearable, point out the oil gland to the left of each hair. Explain that the oil keeps their skin *waterproof* (water can't soak in) and smooth, and their hair shiny. Use the eyedropper to put a droplet of water on the back of children's hands. What happens? (*The water beads up or rolls off. Because skin is waterproof, water does not soak in.*)

5. Tell children that skin covers the entire body like a wrapper, and keeps out harmful germs and dirt. This is why, when children get a scrape or cut, causing some of the skin's top layer to come off, it is important to use soap and water to wash away germs. A scab then forms on that spot giving new skin time to grow.

6. Talk about skin's connection to the sense of touch. On chart paper, copy the poem below. Read the poem aloud once and then reread it, inviting children to read along with you. Then pass around different textured objects and give children time to describe how they feel.

7. Optional: Have children put on their Brain Hats and remind them that the brain helps us figure out what the skin is feeling.

Finger Wise

My fingers tell me oh-so much
through my amazing sense of touch.

I know what's lumpy,
smooth, or bumpy—
what is cold or hot.
I know when something's prickly.
I know when something's not.

Fuzzy, furry, shiny, grainy,
warm and cuddly, icy, rainy.

All this I sense without my eyes
because my fingers are so wise!

—Mary Sullivan

24

Naïve Conceptions

Because we use our fingers so much for our sense of touch, children may not connect the rest of their skin with this sense. Help children think of other ways they feel with their skin, for example, rain on their faces, hot sand on their bare feet, and of course, itches and tickles!

···● ● **Explore** More! ● ●···

Keep Cool!

Our skin performs another important function: it helps regulate our body temperature. Help children feel for themselves how sweat helps cool them off when they get too hot. Have each child wet the back of one hand with water. Tell them that this represents sweat on our skin. Have each of them leave the other hand dry. This represents our skin if we didn't sweat. Tell them to blow gently on both hands. Which hand feels cooler? (*the wet hand*)

Fingerprint Patterns

Let children explore their fingerprints with this activity. First provide them with hand lenses to examine their fingertips. What do they see? (*lines, loops, swirls*) Then tell them that they are going to get a better look at their fingerprints—patterns on the tips of their fingers. Let children take turns dabbing a thumb onto water-based ink pads and stamping the print onto a piece of paper. Afterward, invite children to compare their prints. How are they alike and different? Tell children that no two people have exactly the same fingerprint!

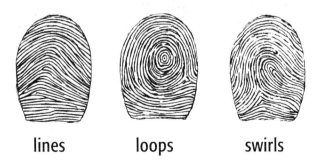

lines   loops   swirls

Explore and celebrate the diversity of hair and skin color with these excellent books:

All the Colors of the Earth by Sheila Hamanaka (HarperTrophy, 1999)

All the Colors We Are/Todos los colores de nuestra piel: The Story of How We Get Our Skin Color by Katie Kissinger (Red Leaf Press, 1994)

Black Is Brown Is Tan by Arnold Adoff (HarperCollins, 1992)

The Colors of Us by Karen Katz (Henry Holt, 1999)

Hairs/Pelitos by Sandra Cisneros (Dragonfly, 1997)

Help children learn more about the characteristics and functions of their skin and hair with these titles:

Hair by Lola Schaefer (Heinemann Library, 2003)

I Can Tell by Touching by Carolyn Otto (HarperCollins, 1994)

Your Skin and Mine by Paul Showers (HarperCollins, 1991; revised)

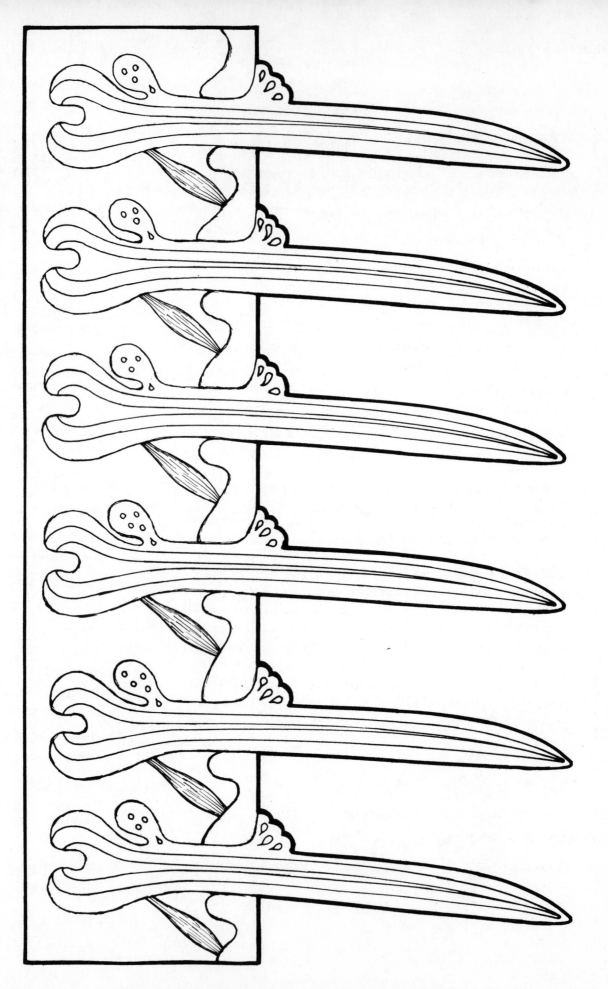

Backbone Streamer

Children make attachable "streamers" that illustrate the backbone and introduce the skeleton.

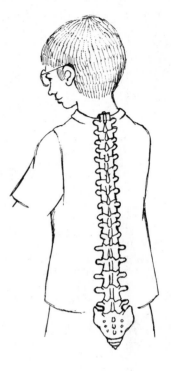

Body Basics for the Teacher

❋ There are more than 200 bones in the human body. Most adults have 206 bones. Children have a few more, which fuse together as children grow. All of the bones make up the *skeleton*.

❋ The skeleton helps hold us up, gives us shape, protects soft parts, like the heart and lungs, and provides an anchor for muscles.

❋ The backbone (or spine) extends from the bottom of the skull to the hipbone. It is composed of 26 bones called *vertebrae*.

❋ The backbone also provides protection for the *spinal cord*. This rope of nerves runs through holes in the vertebrae and carries messages to and from the brain all over the body. The spinal cord is connected to the brain by the *brain stem*.

Materials

❋ Backbone Streamer patterns, page 30

❋ scissors

❋ tape

❋ paper clip

❋ red yarn, about 16 inches long

❋ crayons, colored pencils, or markers (optional)

❋ Brain Hat, page 10 (optional)

Words to Use

backbone
bones
arms
legs
fingers
toes
spinal cord

Making the Wearable

1. Photocopy page 30. Color if desired. Then cut out the upper and lower backbone pieces. Tape them together as shown.

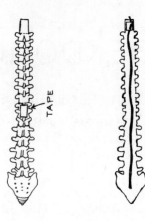

2. Tape one end of the yarn behind the backbone, at the top. This represents the spinal cord. To see the spinal cord, children can lift the backbone.

3. Use a paper clip to attach the top of the Backbone Streamer to the back of each child's collar.

Teaching With the Wearable

1. Before putting on their Backbone Streamers, find out what children know about bones. Ask them what they think is holding their body up.(*bones*) Then invite children to feel some of the bones in their body. Where are some places they can feel them? (*arms, legs, knees, fingers, and so on*)

2. Have children pair up, one behind the other. Tell children to lean forward slightly and then feel the bones in their partners' backbone, from below the neck to just below their waist. Can they feel many small bumps all the way down the middle of their partners' back? Do children think they have one long bone in their back or many bones? (*many bones*)

3. Help children put on their Backbone Streamers and then invite them to examine the wearable on their partner. Point out the bumps running down the center and tell children that these are the bones that make up their backbone.

4. Optional: Have children put on their Brain Hat. Ask children to lift the backbone to see the *spinal cord*. Explain that the spinal cord carries messages to and from the brain all over the body. It helps the brain tell the rest of our body what to do. Tell children that the spinal cord actually runs inside of the backbone. It protects the sensitive spinal cord from being hurt.

Body Bits

The largest bone in the human body is the thigh bone. The smallest bone is in the middle ear. It's about the size of a grain of rice!

Building Vocabulary

For children who are ready for more challenging terms, introduce the word *vertebrae* to describe the individual bones in the back.

Naïve Conceptions

Because they cannot see their skeletons, it may be difficult for children to understand that the skeleton is a framework inside the body. To help them better understand this concept, try this: Drop a pullover shirt or sweater on a table. Ask children to describe how it looks. Then put the sweater on a hanger. How has the shape of the sweater changed? Invite children to feel their collarbones through their clothing. How does it feel? How are the hangers like their bones?

···● Explore More! ●···

What Holds You Up?

What if we didn't have skeletons? Help your students find out with this activity. Invite them to use clay to make figures with long thin bodies, arms, and legs. Can they make their figures stand up? (*no*) Challenge children to find a way to make their figures stand up. Have straws, craft sticks, toothpicks, or large pieces of dried pasta on hand. Children can remold their figures around these materials to discover how an internal skeleton adds support to the body.

Bendable Backbone

What if we each had one long backbone instead of 26 separate vertebrae? How would this affect how we move? Help

children find out with this activity. Give each child a straw that has been cut in half and an 8-inch length of yarn. Tell children to thread the yarn through one half of the straw and then to try bending it gently. Does it bend easily? (*no*) Provide scissors and tell children to cut the other half of the straw into smaller pieces. Then have them thread the yarn through the straw pieces. Does the straw bend easily now? (*yes*) Tell children that the cut-up straw pieces are like the small bones in the backbone and the yarn is like the spinal cord that runs through the backbone. Guide children to understand that if we each had one long backbone, we would not be able to curve our backs or bend in different ways. Many separate bones make the backbone flexible.

What I Know About My Bones

Try this activity to assess children's understanding of the skeleton. Share a book that includes pictures of the skeleton (See Book Break, right.) Then provide children with black construction paper, white tempera paint, and a variety of sponges cut into long, narrow shapes of different sizes. Ask children to use the sponges and paint to make a picture of how their skeletons look. Observe how well children grasp how the bones of the body go together.

Book Break

The Skeleton Inside You by Philip Balestrino (HarperCollins, 1989; revised) Through simple diagrams and text, students learn how the skeleton protects and shapes the body, how bones look inside, how broken bones mend, and more.

Skeletons, Skeletons! By Katy Hall (Penguin, 1991). Each two-page spread features a riddle and a picture of a skeleton. Children can guess the identity of the subject and then hold the pages up to the light (or turn the page) to see who the skeleton belongs to.

You Can't See Your Bones With Binoculars: A Guide to Your 206 Bones by Harriet Ziefert (Blue Apple Books, 2003) This delightful and humorous book uses colorful illustrations and photos of bone x-rays to introduce the parts of the skeleton.

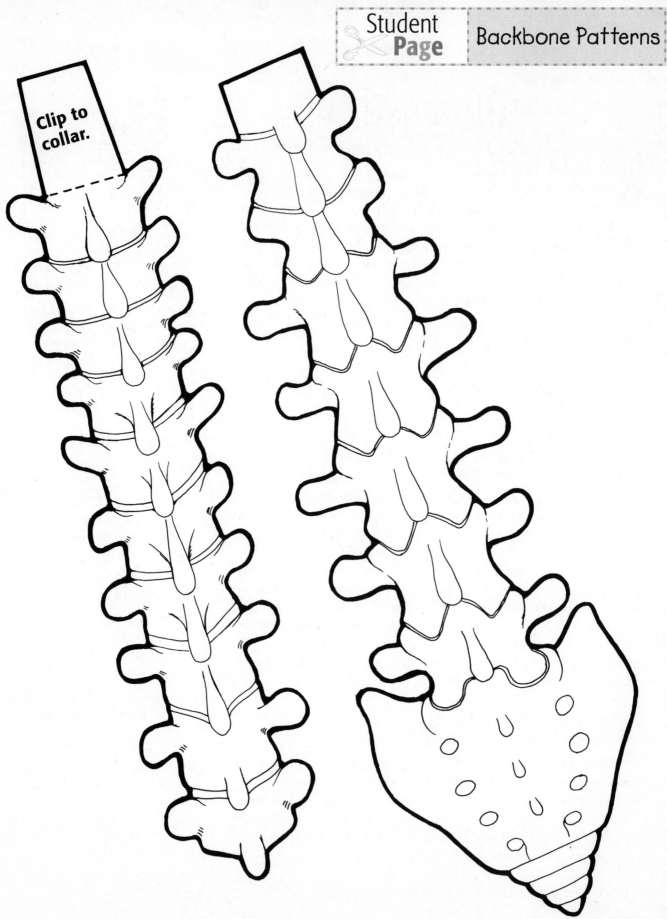

Clip to collar.

Hand Bones Mitt and Ring Set

Children make mitts and rings to learn about the bones in their hands and fingers.

Body Basics for the Teacher

※ With 27 bones each, our hands are the most flexible parts of our bodies.

※ Each hand has a thumb, a shorter digit, composed of two bones, and four other fingers that have three bones each.

※ Bones give hands their shape. They help us pick things up and hold them. The thumb can work with the forefinger (or pointer) to grasp objects. (Monkeys and chimpanzees are the only other animals able to use their thumbs as humans do.)

※ Fingernails are not made of bone. They are made of *keratin*, the same substance that forms hair, feathers, and hooves.

Materials

※ Hand Bones Mitt and Finger Ring patterns, pages 34–35

※ scissors

※ tape

※ crayons, colored pencils, or markers (optional)

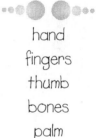

> **Words to Use**
> ●·●● ●·●
> hand
> fingers
> thumb
> bones
> palm
> knuckles
> wrist

Making the Wearable

1. Photocopy pages 34–35. Color the wearables, if desired. Then cut out the mitt and five rings.

2. Tape the tabs on the mitt together as indicated along the left edges.

3. Have students insert their fingers and thumbs through the mitt so it rests comfortably on the right hand as shown.

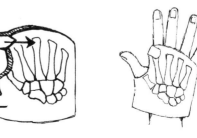

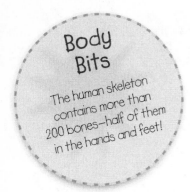

Body Bits

The human skeleton contains more than 200 bones—half of them in the hands and feet!

Building Vocabulary

Help children learn the names for other parts of their hands and fingers, such as *palm*, *knuckles*, and *wrist*.

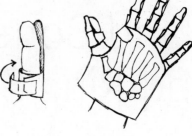

4. Overlap the tabs to make rings that will fit comfortably on each child's fingers. Tape the tabs together. Then have children use their free hands to put on each ring. (NOTE: The finger rings shown on the cover of this book are not positioned on the correct fingers. Use the labels on the tabs to help children match each ring to the corresponding finger.)

Teaching With the Wearable

1. Ask children to talk about ways they use their hands. Ask, "What can you do with your hands and fingers?" (*pick up, hold, and carry things; touch things*)

2. Invite children to feel their free left hands and fingers to compare them with the wearable. "What is on the outside?" (*skin*) Ask children to describe what they notice about it. (*lines on the skin of the palm, wrinkly skin at knuckles, and so on.*) "Does the inside of your hand feel hard or soft?" (*hard*) "What do you think is under the skin?" (*bones*)

3. Encourage students to look at the finger and hand bones on their finger rings and hand mitts. Then tell them to run their fingers over the backs of their left hands. Can they feel the shape of these different bones in their left hands and fingers?

4. Ask children to examine the fingers on their left hands. Discuss ways the fingers are alike and different (*all fingers have bones in them, they all bend, the thumb is shorter and wider than the other four fingers, the four fingers are different lengths*)

5. How many bones does each finger have? Help children count them. Encourage children to bend their fingers to make counting easier. (*the thumb has two bones; the other fingers have three each*)

Naïve Conceptions

Children may not realize that their thumbs look different from their other fingers for a reason. To help them find out more about the structure and function of their thumbs, see Explore More!, What's So Special About Thumbs? on the following page.

●•● ● Explore More! ● ●•●

What's So Special About Thumbs?

Let children try this "hands-on" activity to find out how helpful their thumbs are. Tape children's thumbs to their pointer fingers with masking tape, as shown. Then ask children to try the activities listed below. Afterward, ask, "What activities could you still do easily? Which ones were harder? Did you use other body parts to help you? In what ways do your thumbs help you?"

☼ Clap
☼ Turn the page of a book
☼ Pick up a sheet of paper
☼ Cut with scissors
☼ Write your name

Finger Play Fun

Invite children to explore the many ways in which their fingers can move using the fun poem below. Copy the poem onto chart paper and read it aloud to children. Then invite them to join you on a rereading. On a third reading, encourage children to use their hands and fingers to act out the lines of the poem.

Ten Fingers

I have ten little fingers
and they all belong to me.
I can make them do things,
would you like to see?

I can shut them up tight
or open them wide.
I can put them together,
or make them all hide.

I can make them jump high.
I can make them jump low.
I can fold them quietly
and hold them just so.

—Author Unknown

Book Break

Cleversticks by Bernard Ashley (Dragonfly, 1991) Ling Sung can't write his name, tie his shoes, or button his jacket as well as his classmates can. But when his teacher marvels at his ability to use chopsticks, he discovers that he is good at something after all. Soon everyone in Ling Sung's class wants to be taught how to use chopsticks, too.

My Hands and My Feet by Aliki (HarperCollins, 1992, revised) Perfect for building vocabulary, these two books teach about the anatomy of our hands and feet and also explore the myriad of things we can do with them.

Adorable Wearables That Teach About the Human Body   Scholastic Teaching Resources

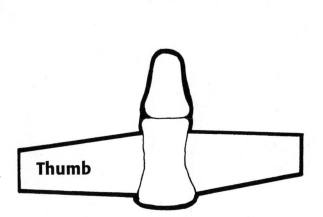

Thumb

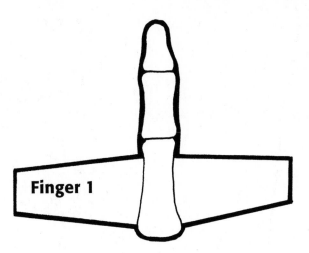

Finger 1

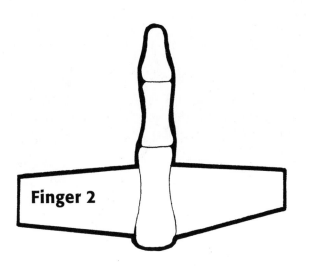

Finger 2

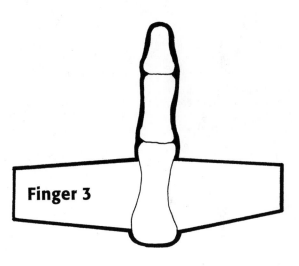

Finger 3

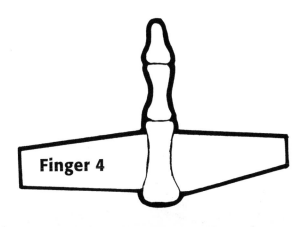

Finger 4

Arm Bones Band

Children explore the bones in their arms and learn about joints.

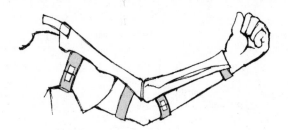

Body Basics for the Teacher

☼ Three long bones make up each arm. There is one upper arm bone and two lower arm bones.

☼ A *joint* is the part of a skeleton where bones meet and fit together. Joints allow the bones in the skeleton to move. In the arm, there is a joint at the elbow, where the upper and two lower arm bones meet. There are also joints at the wrist and shoulder.

Materials

☼ Arm Bones Band patterns, pages 39–40

☼ scissors

☼ tape

Making the Wearable

1. Photocopy pages 39–40.
   Cut out the upper and lower arm bone pieces.

2. Tape them together as shown.

3. Attach the wearable to children's right arms by taping the upper arm bone to the shoulder and the lower arm bones to the wrist.

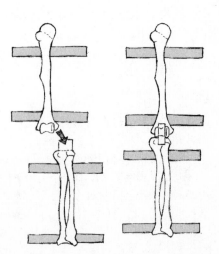

Words to Use

arm
bones
joints
elbow
wrists
knuckles
shoulders
knees
ankles

Teaching With the Wearable

1. Begin the lesson by asking children to describe ways they use their arms. (*to throw a ball, give a hug, swim, pick up and carry things*)

2. Invite children to feel the arm bones in their free arms and compare them with the wearable. Can they feel the shape of these different bones? Ask, "How many bones are in your arm? (*three: one upper arm bone and two lower arm bones*) "What do they look like?" (*long, round or tube-shaped, thicker at the ends*)

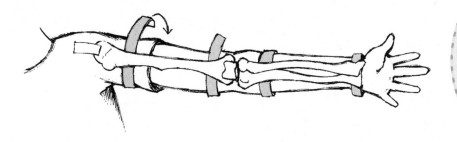

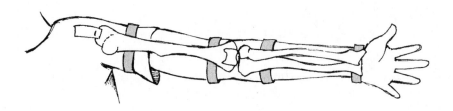

3. Then ask, "Why do you think the arm isn't just one long, straight, bone?" (*because you wouldn't be able to bend it*) Tell children that the point where bones meet and fit together is called a *joint*. Joints between our bones allow them to move. There is a joint where every bone meets another bone. Invite children to locate other joints on their bodies. (*knuckles, wrists, shoulders, knees, ankles*)

4. Let children find out for themselves the important job joints have. Tell them to hold their elbows and knees and stiff, so they don't bend. Then have them try to pick something up, write, or walk. What happens?

Naïve Conceptions

Children may think that there is only one long bone in each part of the arm. Use the wearable to help them understand that the lower arm is made up of two bones.

Body Bits

The elbow is a *hinge joint*. It works like a door hinge that can move forward and backward, but not sideways. Other joints, such as those in the hip, can move in many directions.

Building Vocabulary

Joints allow us to *bend*, *twist*, and *turn*. Encourage children to come up with other words that describe the many ways our joints let us move.

Book Break

How Kids Grow by Jean Marzollo (Scholastic, 1998) Engaging photos of children of different ethnic backgrounds show how children change from birth to age seven.

Arms, Elbows, Hands, and Fingers and *Legs, Knees, Feet, and Toes* by Lola M. Schaefer (Heinemann, 2003) Help young readers build vocabulary and introduce them to the features of nonfiction with these two books. Written in a question-and-answer format, each book includes simple diagrams and bright photos, a table of contents, picture glossary, and index.

···• ● **Explore** More! ● •···

Joint Point Puppets

Invite children to make a jointed puppet and explore the joints in their own bodies.

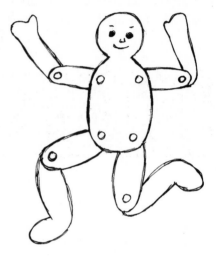

Provide children with large index cards, pencils, scissors, brass fasteners, and crayons or markers. First have children find out where their joints are. Suggest that they start with their heads and move down their bodies. Then tell them they will be making a puppet with joints. What body parts will they need? Tell children to draw and cut out body parts (head, torso, arms, legs, hands, feet, and so on) from the index cards. Then have them use the fasteners to put the puppet's parts together where the joints should go. Invite children to decorate their puppets so they look just like them! As children are playing with their puppets, point out that their puppets' joints move from side to side. Do any of their own joints move in other ways? (*For example, the joints in the shoulders and hips move in almost any direction.*)

Measure Up!

How long are children's bones? Invite them to measure and find out! Give each child a copy of Measure My Bones!, page 41. Then pair up children and give each pair a tape measure. Model for children how to use the tape measure and then help them to measure and record the length of each body part listed on the page.

Naïve Conceptions

Children may not think that their bones are alive and growing. To help them grasp this concept, do the Measure Up! Activity, above, near the beginning of the school year and then repeat it near the end, and have children compare results.

Arm Bones Band Pattern

Tape to shoulder.

upper arm   **Tape around upper arm.**

Tape around arm above elbow.

Adorable Wearables That Teach About the Human Body   Scholastic Teaching Resources

Arm Bones Band Pattern

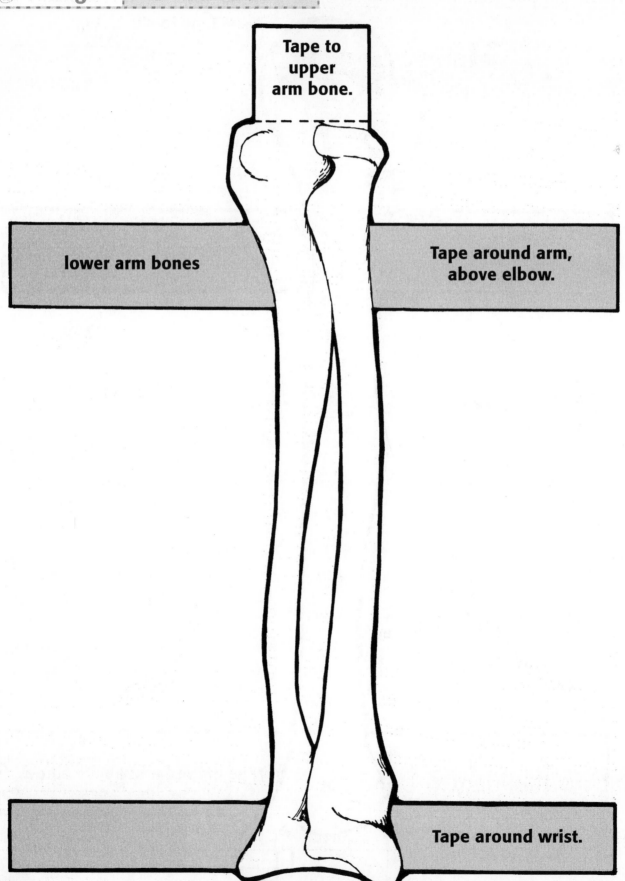

Tape to upper arm bone.

lower arm bones

Tape around arm, above elbow.

Tape around wrist.

Name _____

Measure My Bones

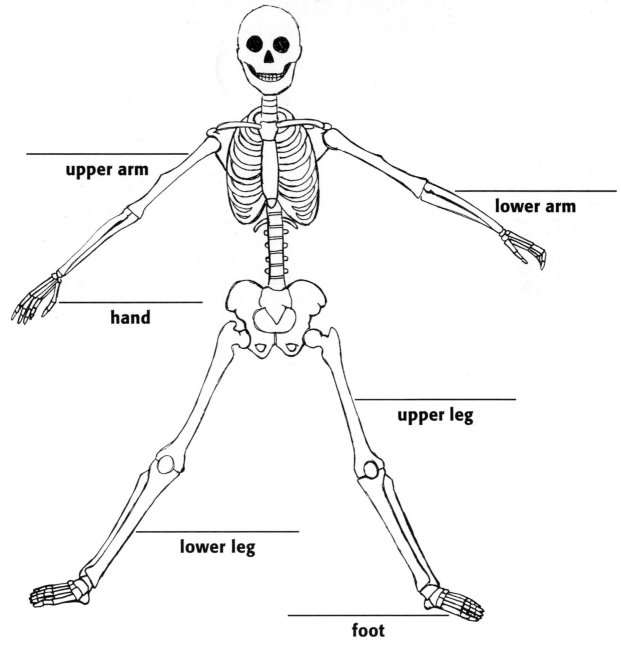

upper arm _____

lower arm _____

hand _____

upper leg _____

lower leg _____

foot _____

Which is the longest bone you can find? _____

Which is the shortest? _____

Muscle Sleeve

Children slip on muscle sleeves and observe muscles in action.

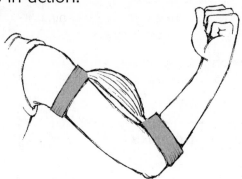

First Facts

☼ There are more than 600 *muscles* in the body. The *brain* sends messages to muscles to move. We rely on our muscles for every move we make.

☼ Most muscles attach to the bones they move. They are called *skeletal muscles*.

☼ Skeletal muscles work by *contracting* (shortening and thickening), then relaxing (returning to their original length and thickness). When skeletal muscles contract they pull on bones and move them.

☼ When we "make a muscle," the upper arm muscle (the *biceps*) contracts. As it shortens and thickens into a bulge, it bends the elbow and pulls the lower arm bones up toward the upper arm bone.

☼ Besides skeletal muscles, there are *smooth* and *cardiac* muscles. These muscles work on their own, without conscious control of the brain. Smooth muscles are found in body parts such as the esophagus and stomach. Cardiac muscles, that make up the heart, contract and relax continuously and automatically.

Materials

☼ Muscle Sleeve pattern, page 45

☼ scissors

☼ tape

☼ crayons, colored pencils, or markers (optional)

☼ Brain Hat, page 10 (optional)

Making the Wearable

1. Photocopy page 45. Color the muscle pattern, if desired. Then cut it out.

2. Have a child extend his or her arm so that the inside of the arm is turned up. Wrap one strip around the child's upper arm, near the shoulder, and tape as shown.

3. Wrap the other strip around the forearm, just below the elbow, and tape as shown.

4. When the child raises his or her forearm, the "muscle" on the wearable will bulge.

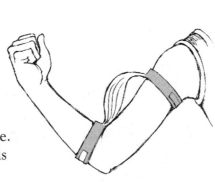

(NOTE: The Muscle Sleeve shown on the cover of this book is positioned farther down the arm than it should be. It also reflects an earlier version of this wearable.)

Body Bits
It takes 43 muscles to frown, but only 15 to smile!

Teaching With the Wearable

1. Ask children what they think muscles do. (*Muscles do work in our bodies. They give us strength to do things such as lift and carry, walk and run, and push and pull; they also pull on bones to help them move.*) Then ask children to find places in their bodies where they can feel muscles working when they perform certain actions. (*pulling in and pushing out the stomach, squinting the eyes, smiling, standing on tiptoe makes a muscle in the lower part of the back of the leg, and so on*)

2. Help children put on their Muscle Sleeves. Then invite children to examine them. Point out where the muscle connects to the bone on the wearable.

3. Have children make fists and bend their other arms at the elbow, feeling the muscle in the upper arm as they do this. "How is your muscle changing shape?" (*It gets bigger, bulges, and feels harder.*)

4. Now have children bend the arms with the Muscle Sleeves in the same way. What happens to the muscle on their models? (*It bulges.*) "What happens when you relax the arm?" (*The muscle flattens to its original shape.*)

Building Vocabulary

If your students are ready, introduce additional vocabulary. Tell them that the muscle in the upper arm is called the *biceps* muscle. When the muscle bulges, we say it *contracts*. When it flattens, we say it *relaxes*.

43

Book Break

The Busy Body Book: A Kid's Guide to Fitness by Lizzy Rockwell (Crown, 2004) This exuberant book describes the importance—and fun—of physical activity to keep the body healthy and strong.

You Can't Make a Move Without Your Muscles by Paul Showers (HarperCollins, 1982) Check your library or online sources for this out-of-print title that provides an introduction to muscles and how they work.

5. To assess children's understanding, ask them to use their observations of the wearables to explain what is happening to the muscles in their arms when they bend their elbows.

6. Optional: Invite children to don their Brain Hats. Ask children to consider the first thing that must happen when you want to move a muscle. (*A message travels from your brain to the muscle telling it to pull on a bone and move it.*)

Naïve Conceptions

Children may believe that exercise gives them more muscles. In fact, exercise strengthens the muscles they already have, but does not add more.

··●● **Explore** More! ●●··

Muscle Power Hokey Pokey

Explain to students that exercise helps their muscles grow strong. (It also helps the rest of the body stay fit.) Reinforce this idea (and get their muscles moving!) by playing the Hokey Pokey game with your class, but replace the words "You do the hokey pokey" with "You use your muscle power!" To play, have children gather in a circle. Help children build vocabulary and directionality by inviting them to suggest different body parts to include, such as *left leg, right arm, left knee, whole self,* and so on.

You put your [body part] in You put your [body part] out You put your [body part] in	*Swing the named body part to the center of the circle, then back out from the center.*
And you shake it all about.	*Wiggle that body part.*
You use your muscle power and you turn yourself around	*Walk a small circle in place as you hold your right elbow in your left palm and wag the right index finger, then switch hands.*
That's what it's all about!	*Face the center, wave hands in front of you; clap on "about."*

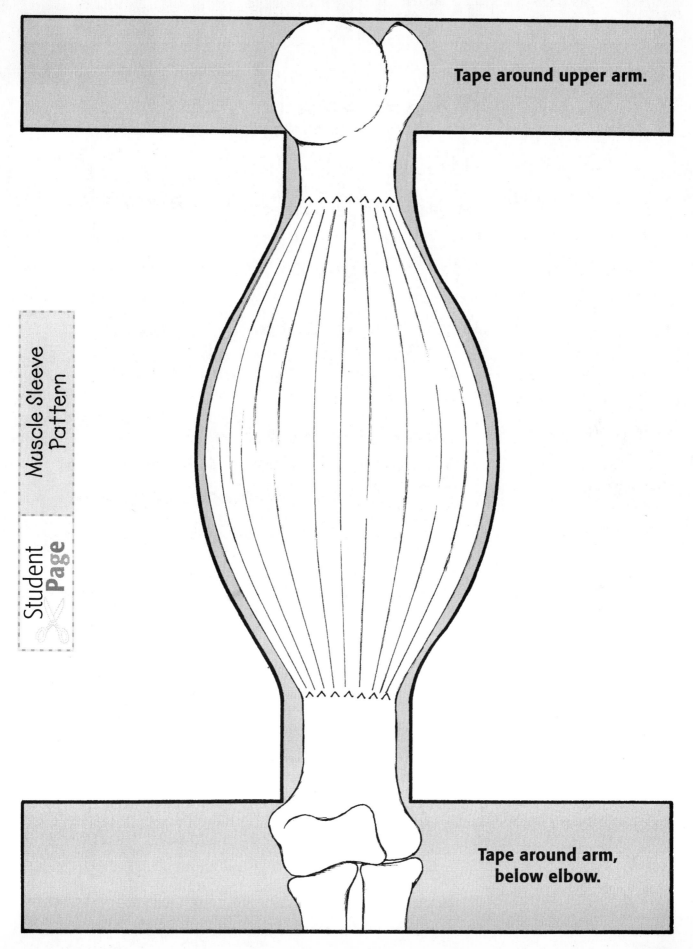

Tape around upper arm.

**Tape around arm,
below elbow.**

Muscle Sleeve
Pattern

Student
Page

Chest Vest

Children make vests to help them learn about the heart, lungs, and ribcage. (This activity is good to do over several days.)

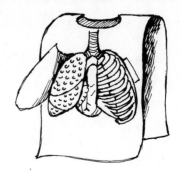

Body Basics for the Teacher

☀ The *heart* is a muscle that contracts and relaxes every second or so. This is our *heartbeat*. When the heart beats, it pumps *blood* throughout the body.

☀ The blood reaches all cells, delivering *oxygen* and *nutrients* to them. It carries away *carbon dioxide* and other wastes.

☀ The heart pumps oxygen-poor blood to the *lungs* to dispose of carbon dioxide and pick up fresh oxygen from the air we breathe. The heart then pumps the oxygen-rich blood from the lungs to all the other parts of the body.

☀ When we breathe in, we pull air through the nose and mouth, down the *windpipe*, and down into the two lungs. When we breathe out, we get rid of the waste carbon dioxide.

☀ Under the lungs is a big muscle called the *diaphragm*. It is the main muscle that helps us breathe in and out. (For simplicity, the diaphragm is not shown on the model.)

☀ The *ribcage* protects internal organs such as the heart and lungs. It is made of 12 pairs of bones that have muscles between them.

Materials

☀ heart, lungs and windpipe, and ribcage patterns, pages 51–53

☀ brown paper grocery bags or 16- by 36-inch sheets of brown craft paper

☀ scissors

☀ tape

☀ assorted crayons, colored pencils, or markers (optional)

☀ paper towel tube (for each student pair)

Body Bits

On average, the heart beats 70 times per minute for humans—that's more than 100,000 beats each day.

Words to Use

heart

heartbeat

pumps

blood

oxygen

nutrients

Day 1: Vest and Heart

Making the Wearable

1. Photocopy pages 51–53 and cut out the four patterns. Set aside the patterns for the lungs and windpipe and the ribcage for Days 2 and 3.

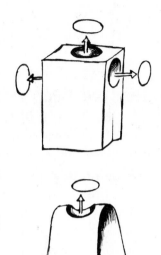

2. Use paper bags or brown craft paper to create "ponchos" for students. If using grocery bags, cut a hole for the head in the bottom as well as armholes in the sides. If using a sheet of craft paper, fold it in half and cut a hole for the head.

Teaching With the Wearable

1. Pair up children and give each pair a paper towel tube. Ask children if they have ever felt their heartbeats. Then tell them tell that they are going to listen to each other's heartbeats. In order to do this, everyone has to be very quiet. Have one child in each pair put one end of the tube to his or her ear and the other end on the partner's chest. Tell the "listeners" to move the tube around until they hear their partner's heartbeat. Have children take turns. Then ask children to describe what they heard. (*a lub-dub sound, a soft drum*)

2. Give a Chest Vest to each child. Now that they have listened to their heartbeats, ask children where on the vest they think their hearts go. Invite them to color their hearts red, if they like. Then help them tape the hearts to the vests in the proper position: slightly left of center on the chest. Then have each child put on his or her vest.

3. Explain that the heart is a muscle that pumps blood every time it squeezes or *beats*. The blood it moves is full of *oxygen* and *nutrients*, which come from the foods we eat. These are things our bodies need to stay healthy. The heart never rests. It pumps night and day, without stopping.

Naïve Conceptions

Children may think the heart is shaped like the classic Valentine's Day symbol. Tell them that the heart actually looks like the picture on the Chest Vest and that it is about the size of a closed fist.

Building Vocabulary

Introduce the word *contracts*. Explain to children that when the heart muscle squeezes or beats, we say it contracts.

Book Break

How Does Your Heart Work? by Don L. Curry (Scholastic Library, 2004) This book offers a simple introduction to the workings of the heart and its important parts. It includes color photos and illustrations, a picture-glossary, and an index.

•••● ● **Explore** More! ●●•••

See Your Heart Beat!

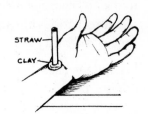

STRAW
CLAY

Feeling the pulse is a concrete way for students to experience their hearts at work. Explain to children that we can also feel our hearts pumping in different places on our bodies, such as our wrists, fingertips, and necks. Children can use this simple device to easily "see" their hearts beating. For each child, stick a two-inch long piece of a straw into a lump of clay about the size of a dime. Have children rest one arm on a table and set the device on the inside of the wrist, near the base of the thumb. Tell them to keep the arm still and watch the straw. It should move slightly with each heartbeat. Ask children to predict how their heartbeats might change after exercise. Invite them to do jumping jacks for 30 seconds and then repeat the activity. What happens to the movement of the straw? (*It moves faster.*) Ask children why they think their heart rates change after exercise. Why is it good to do exercise? (*one reason is to keep our hearts strong*)

Day 2: Lungs

Teaching With the Wearable

Words to Use

•••● ● ●●•••

breathe
air
nose
mouth
chest
oxygen
lungs
windpipe
inhale
exhale

1. Before donning their Chest Vests, ask children to notice how they breathe. Then ask: "How do you take in air?" (*through the nose and mouth*)

2. Have students lay their palms on their chests and take a deep breath in, and then out. Ask: "What happens?" (*Their chest moves out and then in.*) Explain that we breathe air all the time, even when we sleep. That's because we need the *oxygen* in air to live.

3. Give each child his or her Chest Vest and the lung and windpipe pattern. Invite children to color the parts pink, if they like. Explain that when we take in air through the nose or mouth, the air travels down the *windpipe* into the *lungs*. The lungs then fill up with air, like two balloons, and our chests get bigger. When we breathe out, the lungs shrink again, like air going out of the balloons.

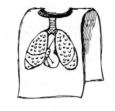

4. Ask children where they think the lungs should go on their vests. Then help them tape the lungs and windpipe to the front of the vest so that the top of the windpipe starts at the hole for the head. The lungs should cover the heart as shown. If not, adjust the position of the heart.

5. Invite children to put on their Chest Vests and then pair up. Ask them to turn to their partner and examine the pictures of the lungs and the windpipe. Have one child trace the path air follows when we breathe in. (*nose or mouth, windpipe, lungs*) The other child can trace the path when we breathe out. (*lungs, windpipe, nose or mouth*)

••• ● **Explore** More! ● •••

Exercise and Breathing

Ask children how they think exercise might affect their breathing. Children may share experiences of "being out of breath" after exercising or of breathing harder. Have children sit quietly and ask them to count how many breaths they take while you time them for 10 seconds. Record children's counts. Then ask children to do jumping jacks or run in place for about 30 seconds. Afterward, repeat the counting process and record the results. Ask: "When did you take more breaths, before or after exercise? Why do you think this is so?" (*When we exercise, our bodies work harder. We need more oxygen to help our bodies work harder.*)

Catch Your Breath!

To help children begin to build an understanding that air takes up space in their lungs, try this: Give each child a paper lunch bag and have him or her breathe normally a few times before taking a deep breath. Tell children to breathe out into the bags, and then pinch the bags closed. Ask them what they think is inside of the bags. (*air*) Explain that the inflated bags show that their lungs can hold a lot of air.

Naïve Conceptions

Because they can't see air, children may have difficulty understanding that air takes up space. Explain that this is the reason our chests expand when we breathe—because air takes up space in our lungs.

49

Day 3: Ribcage

Teaching With the Wearable

1. Give each child the ribcage patterns. Ask children to look at the shape and position of the bones on the pictures. Then ask to feel their own ribs. Can they feel the shape of these bones? Why do they think these bones are called the ribcage? (*looks similar to a bird cage*) Where do they think the ribcage should go on their Chest Vest?

2. Help children place the right and left ribcage pieces over the lungs so they meet. Tape their tabs only to the vest.

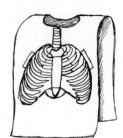

3. Have children lift the flaps on their Chest Vest ribcages to discover the position of the heart and lungs beneath. What does the ribcage protect? (*heart and lungs*)

4. Remind children of the lesson in which they learned about the lungs. (See page 48.) Ask them to breathe in and out and notice how their chests get bigger. Explain that the rib bones have muscles between them. Like other muscles, these squeeze (or *contract*) when we breathe, making our ribs move and allowing our lungs to fill with air. The muscles relax when we exhale.

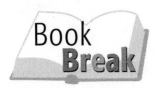

Words to Use

ribcage

bones

heart

lungs

contract

relax

Book Break

Invite young readers to learn more about their lungs by sharing *Breathing* by Ann Sandeman (Copper Beech Books, 1995) and *How Do Your Lungs Work?* by Don L. Curry (Scholastic Library, 2004).

 Explore More!

Measure Up!

Invite children to find out how much their ribcages expand when they take deep breaths—and help them build measurement skills at the same time. Gather two one-yard long pieces of yarn, each in a different color (for each child); scissors; and masking tape. Have each child breathe out. Then use one piece of yarn to measure each child's chest and cut the yarn. Next, have each child inhale deeply. Then remeasure using the other color of yarn. On a bulletin board, tack up and label each child's two lengths of yarn. Invite children to compare them. What similarities and differences do they see among the class's results? Extend the activity by helping children use a yardstick to measure and record the length of their yarn pieces.

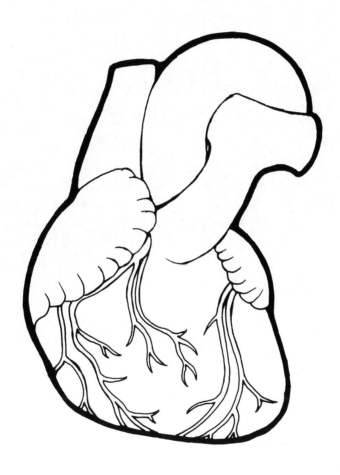

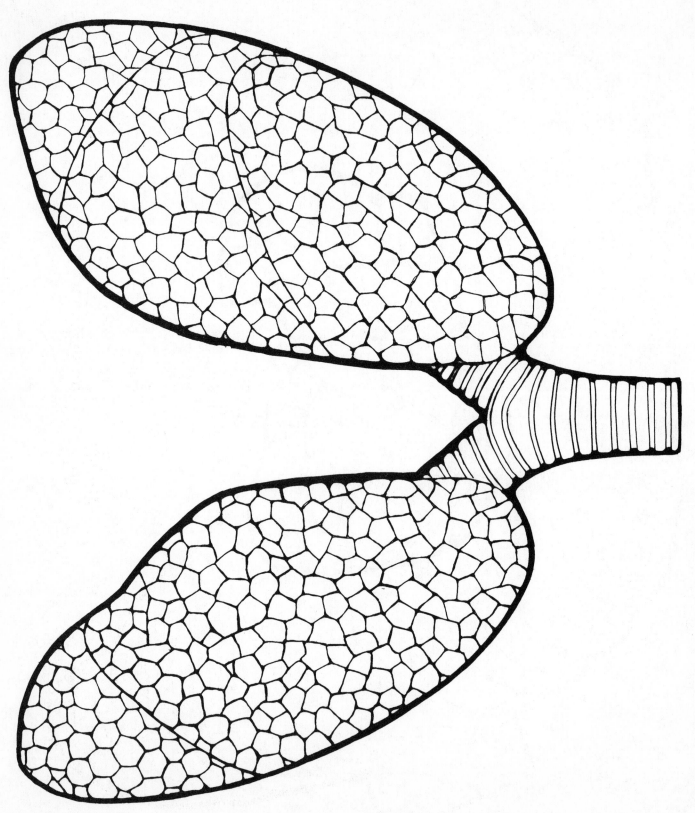

Adorable Wearables That Teach About the Human Body   Scholastic Teaching Resources

Student **Page**

Ribcage Patterns

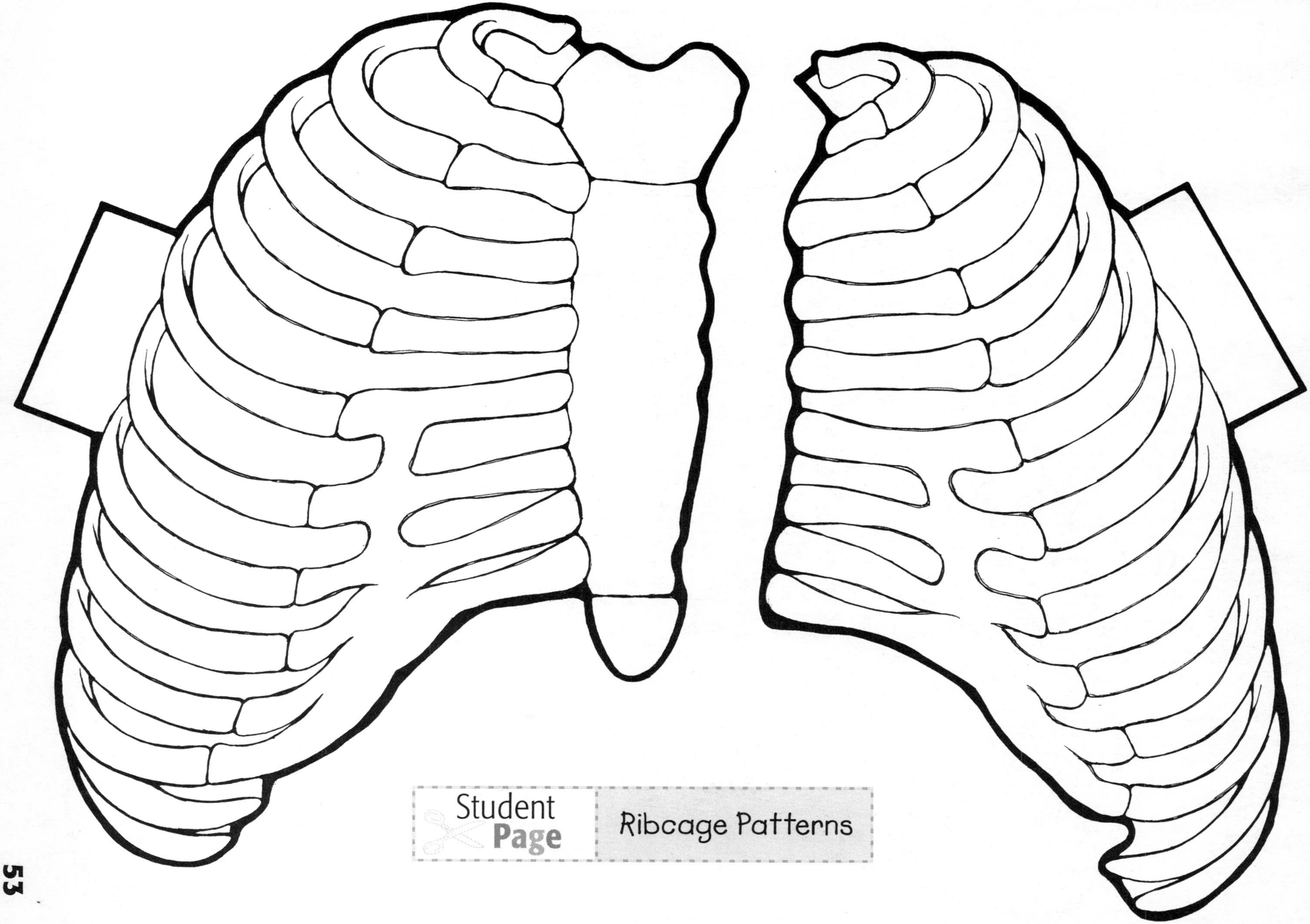

Teeth-and-Tongue Puppet

Children make hand puppets to get a close-up look at their teeth and tongues, and learn that digestion starts in the mouth.

Body Basics for the Teacher

* Our bodies must break down food so we can use its nutrients for energy. This process is *digestion*.

* The teeth begin the process of digestion by tearing, crushing, and mashing food into small pieces. *Saliva* in our mouths helps to moisten and soften food. Chemicals in saliva help break it down more.

* Young children start out with 20 baby teeth. When they are five to seven years old, these teeth start to fall out and 32 permanent teeth begin to replace them.

* A tooth's outer layer, the *enamel*, is the hardest material in the human body. *Dentin*, the hard layer beneath the enamel, protects the soft *pulp* containing nerves, inside the tooth. The *root*, which lies under the gums, anchors the tooth in a socket in the jawbone.

* The *tongue* mashes food and pushes small balls of it to the *throat*.

* The tongue's surface is covered with about 10,000 *taste buds*. The taste buds identify the foods we eat as *salty*, *sour*, *bitter*, or *sweet*.

* *Nerves* in the tongue send messages to the brain which figures out what food we are eating.

Materials

* Teeth-and-Tongue Puppet patterns, page 57
* scissors
* tape
* hand mirrors

Words to Use

digestion
mouth
teeth
chew
saliva
throat
baby teeth
permanent teeth
tongue
taste buds
salty
sour
bitter
sweet

Making the Wearable

1. Photocopy page 57. Cut out the two patterns along the outer solid lines.

2. Cut slits in the mouth pattern along the two thick solid lines.

3. Fold the mouth pattern in half along the vertical dotted line so that the pictures face out. Tape the open edges closed.

4. Fold down the tab on the tongue and tape it inside the mouth.

5. Fold the mouth in half along the horizontal dotted line so that the mouth can close.

6. To wear the puppet, have each child carefully slip the four fingers of one hand into the top slit on the back of the puppet, and the thumb of the same hand into the bottom slit.

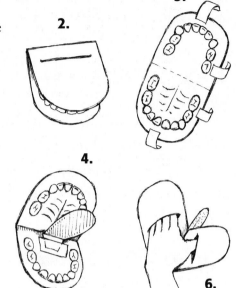

Teaching With the Wearable

1. Begin the lesson by asking children why they think their teeth are important. (*Teeth chew and break down food into small pieces so that we can swallow it.*)

2. Give each pair of children a hand mirror. Ask them to take turns examining their teeth in the mirror and then describe them. Ask, "Are all of your teeth the same?" (*no*) "How are they different?" (*Some teeth are pointy and sharp, while others have a flat, broad surface; teeth are mostly white but may vary in color.*)

3. Ask children to stick out their tongues and look at them in the mirror. What does the tongue look like? (*pink or whitish-pink with little bumps on its surface*)

4. Invite children to color the inside of their puppets based on the observations they made of their own teeth and tongues. Then have them put on their puppets.

5. Explain to children that the teeth on the puppet are shown from above. (To help children make the connection between the drawings of the teeth on their puppets and their own teeth, let them take turns looking into each other's mouths from above.)

Building Vocabulary

Help children learn words related to dental hygiene by discussing the importance of brushing and flossing teeth regularly. Explain to children that bits of food left on our teeth after eating can cause harmful *tooth decay*. Discuss how using a *toothbrush*, *toothpaste*, and *dental floss* can keep teeth healthy.

Book Break

Arthur's Tooth by Marc Brown (Little, Brown, 1987). Arthur's classmates have all lost at least one of their baby teeth. So when is Arthur's coming out?

How Many Teeth? by Paul Showers (HarperCollins, 1991; revised) Readers find out how many teeth babies, toddlers, kids, and adults have, then learn how permanent teeth replace baby teeth.

Little Bear Brushes His Teeth by Julia Langreuter (Millbrook Press, 1997). When Little Bear refuses to brush his teeth, Mama Bear comes up with a clever idea that helps him learn how much fun—and good for him—brushing can be.

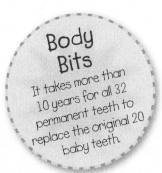

Body Bits
It takes more than 10 years for all 32 permanent teeth to replace the original 20 baby teeth.

6. Then ask, "How many teeth does the puppet have?" Help children count. (*20 in all—10 in the top row and 10 in the bottom*). Explain that young children start out with twenty baby teeth. When they are five to seven years old, these teeth start to fall out, one at a time, and 32 permanent teeth begin to take their place. Invite children to share experiences they may have had losing teeth.

7. Direct children's attention to the tongue on the puppet. Guide them to notice the many small bumps. Explain that these dots are called *taste buds*. They work with our brain to help us figure out the tastes of different foods that we eat. The tongue also helps mash up food, making it easier to swallow, and pushes small bits of food to the throat so we can swallow them.

Naïve Conceptions

Because they lose their baby teeth, children may not realize that the teeth that replace them are permanent. They also may not understand the importance of taking care of their baby teeth. Early decay can harm permanent teeth even before they come in. Good early dental hygiene sets the stage for healthy teeth and gums that will last a lifetime.

Explore More!

Teeth at Work

Help children discover that different teeth serve different functions—biting and chewing—and that digestion begins in the mouth. Children will need hand mirrors, an apple, green and blue crayons, and their Teeth-and-Tongue Puppets. Ask each child to take a bite of an apple. Which teeth—front or back—did the biting? Have children use green crayons to color the corresponding teeth on the puppets. Then direct children to chew and swallow the piece of apple. Which teeth—front or back—did the chewing? Have them color those teeth blue on the puppets. Wrap up by asking children which teeth were better "biters" and which were better "chewers." (*Our sharp, biting front teeth help us to tear or bite off pieces of food. The flat molars in the back help to crush food.*) Which teeth do most of the work when we eat? (*the flat molars*) Finally, have each child take another bite of the apple and chew it thoroughly for about 30 seconds. Ask each child to describe how the apple in his or her mouth has changed. (*It is now soft and very mushy.*) Guide children to understand that, during digestion, food changes so the body can use it for energy. Digestion begins in the mouth when we chew our food.

Teeth-and-Tongue
Puppet Patterns

Digestion Necktie

Children make neckties to learn about
the parts of the digestive system and how they work.

Body Basics for the Teacher

☼ We need food to stay alive, healthy, and to grow. Food contains *nutrients*—proteins, sugars, fats, vitamins, minerals, and water—that give us energy and help us grow.

☼ Our bodies must break down food so we can use its nutrients. This process is *digestion*.

☼ Digestion starts in the mouth. We chew food to break it into bits. Saliva softens it. The tongue then pushes food to the throat.

☼ After swallowing, the chewed food moves down the *food tube*, or *esophagus*. Muscles in the esophagus squeeze the food down into the stomach.

☼ Muscles and powerful juices in the stomach mash and break down the food even more and turn it into a paste like mashed potatoes.

☼ The stomach then squeezes the paste into the coiled-up *small intestine*. There, more juices mix with the food until it is completely broken down. The parts of the food that the body can use are absorbed into the bloodstream.

☼ The unusable parts of food move into the *large intestine* where we release them from the body as solid waste.

☼ Liquid waste is filtered from the blood by the *kidneys* (not shown on the model), and is released from the body as *urine*.

Materials

☼ esophagus, stomach and small intestine, and large intestine patterns, pages 62–65

☼ paper grocery bag or craft paper

☼ scissors

☼ tape

☼ paper clips

☼ crayons, colored pencils, or markers (optional)

Words to Use

food
nutrients
digestion
mouth
teeth
saliva
food tube
stomach
small intestine
large intestine
waste

Making the Wearable

1. Photocopy pages 62–65. Color the parts of the digestive system, if desired. (To help children distinguish between the different parts, color each differently.)

2. Cut out the pieces on pages 62–65.

3. Cut out a necktie shape from a paper grocery bag as shown.

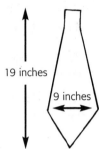

19 inches

9 inches

4. Roll the esophagus (food tube) rectangle into a cylinder so the edge overlaps the white section on the dotted line. Tape the tube together.

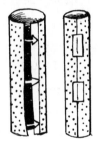

5. Tape the top and bottom of the food tube to the necktie. Both ends of the food tube should remain open.

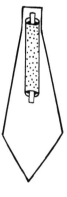

6. Tape the stomach to the end of the food tube as shown.

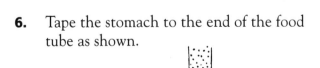

7. Tape the small intestine to the end of the stomach.

59

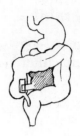

8. Tape the large intestine on top of the small intestine as shown. Then secure to the tie using tape.

9. Tuck the top of the necktie into children's collars. Use paper clips or tape to hold the ties in place.

Teaching With the Wearable

1. Begin by asking children to describe what they think happens to food after they chew and swallow it. Then tell them that they are going to learn about digestion—how our body breaks down food so that we can use it to stay alive, for energy, and to help us grow.

2. Help children put on their Digestion Neckties. Then pair up children and invite them to begin tracing on each other's necktie the path of food as it moves from the mouth. Point out that food first goes through the *food tube* which squeezes it down to the *stomach*.

3. Explain that the stomach is like a bag that expands to hold the food we eat. It also works like a blender to stir and mix up it up. Stomach juices help to turn the food into a paste that is similar to mashed potatoes. Invite children to use their hands to pretend to mash up food.

4. The paste then moves to the *small intestine*, which is shaped like a long, coiled-up rope. There, powerful juices mix with the food and break it down even more so the body can use it.

5. Tell children that we cannot digest all of the foods that we eat. The parts of food that our bodies cannot use move on to the *large intestine*. When we go to the bathroom, this waste, including some water, leaves the large intestine and passes out of the body. Explain that because the waste contains germs, it is important to wash our hands after using the bathroom.

Building Vocabulary

Tell children that the word *esophagus* is the name for the food tube that leads from their mouth to their stomach.

Body Bits

The food you eat takes one to two days to move from one end of the digestive system to the other.

Naïve Conceptions

Some children believe that the foods they eat retain their original forms after swallowing. For example, a child may think that when he or she eats a banana, a banana shape will end up in his or her stomach. To help dispel this thinking, do the Digestion Mash activity on the next page.

Explore More!

The Big Squeeze

Students may think that once food is chewed, it simply drops down to the stomach. Help them understand *peristalsis* —the wavelike action in the food tube (esophagus) that pushes food down to the stomach. Tightly wad up quarter pages of paper so they just fit in the tops of the food tubes on children's Digestion Neckties. Tell children that the wads of paper represent pieces of food they have swallowed. Invite each child to squeeze the "food" down his or her tube by pinching the tube until the paper reaches the stomach.

Digestion Mash

To help children better understand how foods break down during digestion, try these simple activities:

☀ Drop a cracker into a glass of water. Then break up another cracker into a second glass of water. Tell children that the crumbled cracker represents food that has been chewed by our teeth. Ask them to describe what happens to the cracker in each glass. (*They both soften and fall apart, but this happens more quickly with the crumbled cracker.*)

☀ At snacktime, give each child a banana, a bowl, and a fork. Ask children to peel the bananas, break them into pieces in the bowls, and then use the forks to mash up the bananas. Explain that this is like what happens to foods in our stomachs. Then give each child a graham cracker on which to spoon his or her nutritious banana mash.

Intestines, End to End

Help children visualize just how long the coiled-up intestine is. Head outdoors and mark a distance of 16 feet (about the length of a five- or six-year old child's small intestine) with yarn. Explain to children that the yarn shows the length of the small intestine if it were to be stretched out. Extend the activity by asking children to estimate how long *your* small intestine is (about 22 feet). Then measure and cut yarn to this length and compare.

Book Break

Bread and Jam for Frances by Russell Hoban (HarperCollins, 1964) Frances discovers that there's a downside to eating her favorite, bread and jam, for every meal! Use this classic story to discuss the importance and appeal of a varied, balanced diet.

Good Enough to Eat: Kids' Guide to Food and Nutrition by Lizzy Rockwell (HarperCollins, 1999) In this book, children learn the basics of good nutrition and the importance of its role in maintaining a healthy body. Healthy food suggestions appear throughout.

Why Does My Tummy Rumble When I'm Hungry?: and Other Questions About Digestion by Sharon Cromwell (Heinemann Library, 1998). This book answers the title question as well as others kids are curious about such as, "What is a burp?" and "Why does my mouth water?"

Esophagus
(Food Tube) Pattern

Stomach Pattern

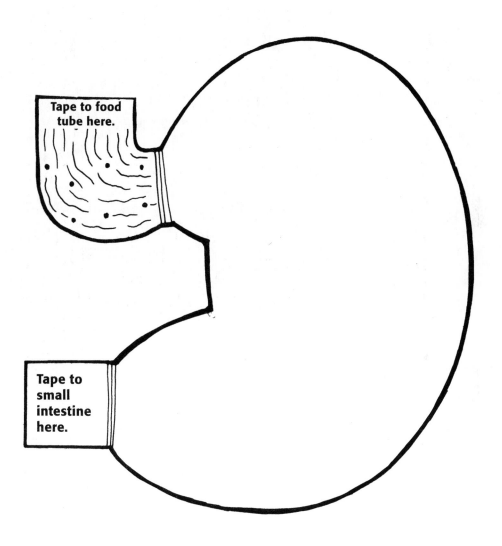

Tape to food tube here.

Tape to small intestine here.

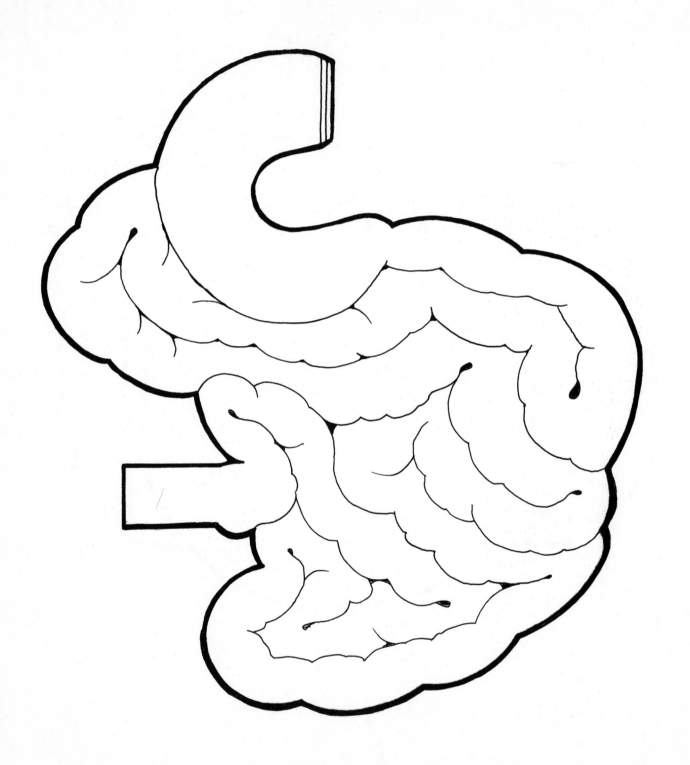